Nothing but Trouble

The Story of Althea Gibson

by Sue Stauffacher

illustrated by Greg Couch

Alfred A. Knopf ✦ New York

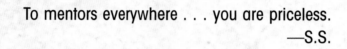

To mentors everywhere . . . you are priceless.
—S.S.

For Marilyn
—G.C.

Althea Gibson was the tallest, wildest tomboy in the history of Harlem. Everybody said so.

Her mama said: Just give that child a nickel for a loaf of bread and see what happens. Soon as she catches sight of those boys playing stickball, my bread is long forgotten.

Her daddy said: That girl stays out so late playing basketball, she doesn't even come home some nights.

Her teacher said: Half the time she doesn't even return from recess. I'd see a lot more of Althea if I taught lessons on the playground.

The policeman said: She's a fast runner, all right, but you can't make a sport out of nickin' sweet potatoes. That's against the law.

They all said: Althea Gibson,
you're nothing but trouble!

Althea didn't care what they said.
She knew she would be somebody someday.
Somebody big, like Charlie Parker
or Sugar Ray. In the meantime,
just one thing to care about in this world:
The Game.

Give her a stick,

a paddle,

a hoop,

or a ball,
and Althea Gibson
was good to go.

Buddy Walker was the play leader down on
143rd Street, where Althea lived. At night,
he was a musician in one of Harlem's society
orchestras. When Buddy watched Althea play
paddle tennis, he didn't see "nothing but trouble."
No, sir, except maybe for the poor rubber ball.
What he saw in Althea was pure possibility.

Times were hard, but Buddy scrounged up enough money to buy Althea a stringed tennis racket at a secondhand store. It didn't look like much next to the big wooden paddle Althea normally used for street tennis.

After she practiced a little, Buddy asked a friend at the Harlem River Tennis Courts to play a few sets with her. As Althea covered the court, Buddy forgot all about the wild tomboy who roamed the streets of Harlem.

What Buddy saw was music in the way she moved.

Buddy wasn't the only one. Other players stopped their games to get a look at her. Althea saw the other players watching her. It felt good. Made her feel like she was somebody.

"Althea," Buddy said after the game, trying to contain his excitement. "This is Juan Serrell, a friend of mine. We have an idea."

Juan Serrell belonged to the Cosmopolitan, the ritziest tennis club in Harlem. All the Sugar Hill society people belonged there. "You play tennis here," Buddy told Althea, "you can make something of yourself."

After the members of the club saw what Althea
could do, Buddy and Juan convinced
a few of them to pay for lessons
with the club's one-armed tennis pro,
Fred Johnson. Fred tried to improve Althea's ways,
on and off the court. While Althea loved
playing a new game on a big fancy court,
she didn't like being told how to act.

"Never said I wanted to be a fine lady,"
she complained to Buddy.

Unfortunately for her, the members of the
Cosmopolitan didn't like her wild ways either.
They shook their heads and whispered.
Nothing but trouble, that one.

Mrs. Rhoda Smith was a nice society lady
who bought Althea her first tennis outfit, so
she'd look like all the other players on the
court. She made time to play regularly
with Althea and to instruct her in
the polite rules of the sport.

"Now, Althea, when a loose ball rolls onto the court, you don't just bat it out of the way in any old direction. You send it back to the player it belongs to. That's how it's done in court tennis."

"Aw, Mrs. Smith," Althea muttered. "Can't we just play tennis?"

Buddy tried to explain the importance of keeping cool. "You've got to decide, Althea. Are you going to play your game, or are you going to let the game play you? When I go to the jazz club, I play like a tiger, but I wear a tuxedo."

"Hmmmph," Althea said, throwing her tennis racket on the ground. "I don't fit with these rich society folks. I'd rather punch somebody's lights out at Stillman's Gym."

Buddy said, "Althea, I still believe. . . ."

A year later, Althea was in her first real tennis tournament. She played well, but she lost in the finals to Nana Davis.

"After I beat her," Nana told the reporters, "she headed straight to the grandstand without bothering to shake my hand. Some kid had been laughing at her and she was going to throw him out. I tell you, Althea Gibson is nothing but trouble!"

It took time, a good long time, but slowly Althea
learned that wanting to slug her opponent as
soon as she started losing her match made her
a worse tennis player than if she kept her cool.

With Buddy's help, Althea realized she could dress up in white and act like a lady, and still beat the liver and lights out of the ball.

Tennis changed Althea, all right.

But just as importantly . . .

Ever since Miss Gibson
rallied in the second set of the women's finals,
she has proven to be nothing but trouble
for seasoned U.S. and world champ
Louise Brough.

Althea changed tennis.

She did it, ladies and gentlemen!
She did it! Althea Gibson has won
the championship here at
Wimbledon's Centre Court!

With that, Althea Gibson became
the first African American, man
or woman, ever to compete in
and win the coveted Wimbledon Cup,
long considered the highest honor
in tennis.

And she never did forget the man who first
saw the Champion of the World in the
wildest tomboy in Harlem.

"Tonight is the conclusion of a long and satisfying journey.

It all started on one of New York's play streets when

Buddy Walker, a play street supervisor, said,

'Althea, I believe you could become

a good lawn tennis player.'

With those words,

he handed me my first tennis racket.

Tonight I thank Buddy Walker

for a most satisfying victory."

Author's Note

Althea Gibson was born in 1927 into a family of sharecroppers. In 1957, she became the greatest female tennis player in the world. Althea Gibson lived the American dream. But dreams aren't achieved alone. Though this is Althea's story, it is also Buddy Walker's story. When he reached out to a child who was not his own by buying her a tennis racket, Buddy set in motion all the wonderful things to come for Althea, who was always gracious about acknowledging the people who helped her turn her life around: "If I've made it," she wrote, "it's half because I was game to take a wicked amount of punishment along the way and half because there were an awful lot of people who cared enough to help me."

Buddy, Juan Serrell, and Fred Johnson were the first of many influential people—including doctors, teachers, housewives, even boxing greats Sugar Ray Robinson and Joe Louis—who helped Althea achieve her dreams.

But Althea would need even more supporters to help her fight her most insidious foe: racism. She has been called the "Jackie Robinson of tennis" because she was the first black player, man or woman, to break the color barrier and compete and win at Wimbledon.

The only way to reach a competition like Wimbledon is to be invited to play in smaller tournaments. The all-white United States Lawn Tennis Association (USLTA) effectively kept Althea out by not inviting her to tournaments. Their reason? She didn't have enough experience. But how could she get experience if she couldn't play?

When Alice Marble, an influential white tennis player, heard about Althea's predicament, she wrote an article in a tennis magazine insisting Althea be allowed to compete. Ms. Marble wrote that she would be "bitterly ashamed" if the sport to which she had devoted a good part of her life would not allow Althea to play simply because of the color of her skin. "If the field of sports has got to pave the way for all of civilization, let's do it," she wrote. "At this moment tennis is privileged to take its place among the pioneers for a true democracy."

The USLTA was publicly shamed and Althea began to receive invitations. Over the next seven years she competed and won many top tennis honors, including the Wimbledon Cup twice, in 1957 and 1958.

Althea Gibson died on September 28, 2003. If you want to read more about her in her own words, check out one of her excellent, though out-of-print, autobiographies from the library: *I Always Wanted to Be Somebody* and *So Much to Live For*. Or visit www.altheagibson.com.

THIS IS A BORZOI BOOK PUBLISHED BY ALFRED A. KNOPF

Text copyright © 2007 by Sue Stauffacher
Illustrations copyright © 2007 by Greg Couch

All rights reserved.
Published in the United States by Alfred A. Knopf, an imprint of Random House Children's Books, a division of Random House, Inc., New York.

KNOPF, BORZOI BOOKS, and the colophon are registered trademarks of Random House, Inc.

www.randomhouse.com/kids

Educators and librarians, for a variety of teaching tools, visit us at www.randomhouse.com/teachers

Library of Congress Cataloging-in-Publication Data
Stauffacher, Sue.
Nothing but trouble : the story of Althea Gibson / by Sue Stauffacher ;
illustrated by Greg Couch. — 1st ed.
p. cm.
ISBN 978-0-375-83408-0 (trade)
ISBN 978-0-375-93408-7 (lib. bdg.)
1. Gibson, Althea, 1927–
2. African American women tennis players—
Biography—Juvenile literature. I. Title.
GV994.G53S72 2007
796.342092—dc22
(B)
2006012605

The illustrations in this book were created using a combination of acrylic paintings and digital imaging.

PRINTED IN CHINA
August 2007
10 9 8 7 6 5 4 3 2
First Edition

1927

Althea Gibson
is born on a cotton farm
in Silver, South Carolina.

1930

Althea's family moves to
Harlem in New York City.

1949

Althea competes in
the United States Lawn Tennis
Association's (USLTA)
Eastern Indoor Tournament.

1947–1956

Althea wins ten straight
national women's singles
championships in the ATA.

1949

Althea enrolls in college
at Florida A&M, where she
plays on the women's
basketball team and the men's
golf team, in addition to
playing tennis.

1950

Althea reaches the women's
finals of the USLTA
National Championship
(now called the U.S. Open).

1958

Althea retires from amateur
tennis to become a singer,
a professional golf and tennis
player, and the state athletic
commissioner of New Jersey,
among other things.

1957, 1958

Althea wins the women's
USLTA National Championship.